Promises of
GOD'S ABUNDANCE
for a More
Meaningful Life

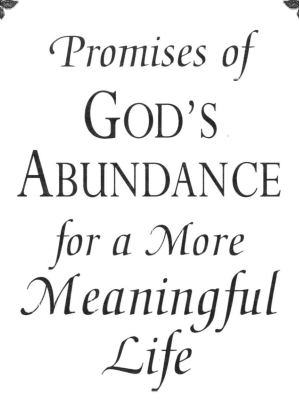

Promises of
GOD'S
ABUNDANCE
for a More
Meaningful
Life

Kathy Collard Miller

STARBURST PUBLISHERS
Lancaster, Pennsylvania

Kathy Collard Miller is the author of 30 books, including the best-selling *God's Vitamin "C" for the Spirit* and *God's Abundance*. She speaks across the nation and internationally. Contact: P.O. Box 1058, Placentia, CA 92871. (714) 993-2654. Kathyspeak@aol.com.

To schedule Author appearances write: Author Appearances, Starburst Promotions, P.O. Box 4123 Lancaster, Pennsylvania 17604 or call (717) 293-0939. Website: www.starburstpublishers.com

CREDITS:
Cover design by David Marty Design
Text design and composition by John Reinhardt Book Design

Unless otherwise noted, or paraphrased by the author, all Scripture quotations are from the New International Version of The Holy Bible.

Scripture taken from the HOLY BIBLE: NEW INTERNATIONAL VERSION®. NIV®. Copyright © 1973, 1978, 1984 by International Bible Society. Used by permission of Zondervan Publishing House. The "NIV" and "New International Version" trademarks are registered in the United States Patent and Trademark Office by the International Bible Society.

Promises of God's Abundance

First Printing, November, 1998
ISBN: 0-914984-09-8
Library of Congress Catalog Number 98-86023
Printed in the United States of America

Contents

Introduction

Our Almighty, loving God has provided an abundance of promises in His Word, which is His personal love letter to each of us. A promise can be defined as an indication of a successful prospect or future and it's the basis for our expecting God to work in and through us.

In God's kingdom, His promises are dependent upon our cooperation and obedience with His plan. Therefore, He lovingly speaks to us saying, "My children, because I know My plan for you, I assure you that if you obey Me, I will do certain things in your life. That is a promise because I love you."

You will find in this little book a wealth of God's promises. When we concentrate on His promises, we enjoy more peace, security, and love—the foundation of a simpler life in our thoughts, motives, and actions. The more we dwell on those beautiful things, the more we'll discover the abundant life Jesus promised in John 10:10.

That's the equation for God's abundance in our lives: claiming God's promises added to simple obedience, equals abundance! I hope you enjoy all those elements of your spiritual inheritance by focusing on the wonderful promises in this book.

KATHY COLLARD MILLER

Disciplining Children

All discipline for the moment seems not to be joyful, but sorrowful; yet to those who have been trained by it, afterwards it yields the peaceful fruit of righteousness.

HEBREWS 12:11 (NASB)

Children aren't going to welcome being disciplined, but later they'll welcome the good character traits that result.

The time to start correcting the children is before they start correcting you.

HOMER PHILLIPS

Whispered Directions

If you go the wrong way—to the right or to the left—you will hear a voice behind you saying, "This is the right way. You should go this way."

Isaiah 30:21 (NCV)

The more we know God intimately, the more clearly we'll hear His whispered guidance.

The Almighty does nothing without reason, though the frail mind of man cannot explain the reason.

Saint Augustine

Facing a Fork in the Road

I will instruct you and teach you in the way you should go; I will counsel you and watch over you.

PSALMS 32:8 (NIV)

Are you facing a fork in the road? Keep your eyes peeled for God's road signs. He promises to guide you.

I praise God because he not only guides my directions but overrules my mistakes.

H. NORMAN PELL

God's Omniscience

The lot is cast into the lap, But its every decision is from the LORD.

PROVERBS 16:33 (NASB)

God is never up in heaven wringing His hands, upset about what has happened on earth. He has always known and always has a plan.

God's knowledge of the future is as complete as is His knowledge of the past and the present, and that, because the future depends entirely upon Himself.

A. W. PINK

Comforting Direction

Yea, though I walk through the valley of the
shadow of death, I will fear no evil: for thou art
with me; thy rod and thy staff they comfort me.

PSALMS 23:4 (KJV)

We may not welcome the disciplinary tools of the
rod and staff, but God patiently redirects us if we
lose our way.

Lord, send me where Thou wilt, only go with me;
lay on me what Thou wilt, only sustain me. Cut any
cord but the one that binds me to Thy cause, to Thy
heart.

TITUS COAN

Feeling Confused?

For God is not a God of disorder but of peace.

1 Corinthians 14:33 (NIV)

If you're feeling confused, don't even begin to think it's from God. He brings peace not turmoil.

Never doubt in the dark what God told you in the light.

V. Raymond Edman

Kept From Stumbling

Do not be afraid of sudden terror, Nor of trouble
from the wicked when it comes; For the LORD
will be your confidence, And will keep your foot
from being caught.

PROVERBS 3:25–26 (NKJV)

When we run scared, we stumble in our faith. Instead, know God promises to give you a confident step as you walk in His way.

When I met Christ at the crossroads of life, he showed me which way to go by walking it with me.

ANONYMOUS

15

Worry Steals Perspective

Commit to the LORD whatever you do, and your plans will succeed.

Proverbs 16:3 (NIV)

Have you ever noticed that worry concentrates on yesterday or tomorrow? Instead, commit today to God and leave the results to Him.

If you have one eye on yesterday and one eye on tomorrow, you'll look at today cross-eyed.

Anonymous

Step By Step Guidance

In his heart a man plans his course, but the
LORD determines his steps.

PROVERBS 16:9 (NIV)

We should make plans as we seek God, knowing
that if we didn't quite hear Him clearly, He'll continue to correct our direction.

God not only orders our steps, He orders our stops.

GEORGE MULLER

Helping Others

*Praise be to the God and Father of our Lord
Jesus Christ, the Father of compassion and the
God of all comfort, who comforts us in all our
troubles, so that we can comfort those in any
trouble with the comfort we ourselves have
received from God.*

2 CORINTHIANS 1:3–4.

Your difficulties are not in vain because whatever
you learn from them, you will be able to pass along
to others. Don't hold back! Share your gems of
comfort!

"Encouragement is oxygen to the soul."

GEORGE M. ADAMS.

New Creature In Christ

Therefore if any man is in Christ, he is a new creature; the old things passed away; behold, new things have come.

2 CORINTHIANS 5:17 (NASB)

We all love fresh starts. When you came to know Jesus personally, you started a new life.

Having given us the package, do you think God will deny us the ribbon?

OSWALD C. J. HOFFMAN

Surrounded By Enemies

*The LORD is my light and my salvation; Whom
shall I fear? The LORD is the defense of my life;
Whom shall I dread? When evildoers came
upon me to devour my flesh, My adversaries
and my enemies, they stumbled and fell. Though
a host encamp against me, My heart will not
fear; Though war arise against me, In spite of
this I shall be confident.*

PSALMS 27:1–3 (NASB)

We've all felt like everybody is against us at times,
but Jesus says He's on our side and we need not
feel alone.

A person can respond to suffering like an egg, or
like a potato. A potato goes into the boiling water
hard, but comes out pliable. An egg goes into the
boiling water soft and comes out hard.

ANONYMOUS

God Understands

*Shout for joy, O heavens; rejoice, O earth; burst
into song, O mountains! For the LORD comforts
his people and will have compassion on his
afflicted ones.*

ISAIAH 49:13 (NIV)

Because of God's merciful nature, He understands
our pain and knows His plan for comforting us.

Stormy weather is what man needs from time to
time to remind him he's not really in charge of anything.

BILL VAUGHAN

God Is Real

And without faith it is impossible to please
God, because anyone who comes to him must
believe that he exists and that he rewards those
who earnestly seek him.

HEBREWS 11:6 (NIV)

If we want to give God joy, all we need to do is believe He's alive.

My most cherished possession I wish I could leave you is my faith in Jesus Christ, for with him and nothing else you can be happy, but without him and with all else you'll never be happy.

PATRICK HENRY

Walking By Sight

We live by faith, not by sight.

When we're walking by sight, we require proof of God's promises. When we're walking by faith, we believe He'll fulfill His promises—even when there isn't immediate evidence.

We are wrong when we say that we must verify God and then we will have faith in him. Faith throws a bridge toward God and finds the divine Reality.

HUGH THOMSON KERR

Do You Require Evidence?

Now faith is the substance of things hoped for,
the evidence of things not seen.

HEBREWS 11:1 (KJV)

If you're feeling like you're out on a limb as you're trusting God for His promise, have no fear. Your faith in God's greatness will keep it attached to the tree.

Faith is a living, daring confidence in God's grace. It is so sure and certain that a man could stake his life on it a thousand times.

MARTIN LUTHER

Watch Out For Those Darts

In addition to all this, take up the shield of faith, with which you can extinguish all the flaming arrows of the evil one.

EPHESIANS 6:16 (NIV)

Living for Christ doesn't mean you won't be fired on. Satan will attack with darts of doubt: Put up your shield and claim God's promises.

Faith makes the uplook good, the outlook bright, the inlook favorable, and the future glorious.

V. RAYMOND EDMAN

God Is Generous

*"Bring the whole tithe into the storehouse, that
there may be food in my house. Test me in this,"
says the LORD Almighty, "and see if I will not
throw open the floodgates of heaven and pour
out so much blessing that you will not have
room enough for it."*

MALACHI 3:10 (NIV)

Want to see your well overflowing? Then prime it
with your own generous giving out of a grateful
heart. Yet keep the right attitude about it.

Money is an article which may be used as a universal passport to everywhere except heaven, and as a
universal provider of everything except happiness.

ANONYMOUS

Generosity Creates Abundance

But this I say: He who sows sparingly will also reap sparingly, and he who sows bountifully will also reap bountifully. So let each one give as he purposes in his heart, not grudgingly or of necessity; for God loves a cheerful giver. And God is able to make all grace abound toward you, that you, always having all sufficiency in all things, may have an abundance for every good work.

2 CORINTHIANS 9:6–8 (NKJV)

If you aren't giving from pure motives, you may not be able to count on getting the blessings you thought. God loves an obedient heart giving from gratitude.

Men make counterfeit money; in many more cases, money makes counterfeit men.

SYDNEY J. HARRIS

Promised Prosperity

My dear friend, I know your soul is doing fine,
and I pray that you are doing well in every way
and that your health is good.

3 JOHN 1:2 (NCV)

Although God's definition of prosperity is different for each one of His children, He wants you to succeed in the specialized plan He's developed just for you.

My inclination is to think that Christ meant it in a very literal way when He said to seek the lower seats. That does not mean, as I see it, that we should refuse the higher if the Lord takes us there, but He should do the taking.

FRANCIS A. SCHAEFFER

Honor God

Fear the LORD, you his saints, for those who fear him lack nothing.

PSALMS 34:9 (NIV)

Money won't make you happy, but honoring God will assure you have everything you truly need. That's true happiness.

The poorest man I know is the man who has nothing but money.

JOHN D. ROCKEFELLER, JR.

Blessings Of Giving

Give, and it shall be given unto you; good
measure, pressed down, and shaken together, and
running over, shall men give into your bosom.
For with the same measure that ye mete withal
it shall be measured to you again.

LUKE 6:38 (KJV)

If you want to be blessed, then give with a generous heart.

Giving to the Lord is but transporting our goods to
a higher floor.

ANONYMOUS

Nothing Bad Enough

*I will cleanse them from all the sin they have
committed against me and will forgive all their
sins of rebellion against me.*

JEREMIAH 33:8 (NIV)

God is eager to jump in with His cleansing forgiveness. He can't wait to hear your request for cleansing.

Don't try to deal with sin, for you are sure to lose. Deal with Christ; let him deal with your sin and you are sure to win.

ARTHUR H. ELFSTRAND

Simple Forgiveness

*If we confess our sins, he is faithful and just
and will forgive us our sins and purify us from
all unrighteousness.*

1 JOHN 1:9 (NIV)

It seems too easy, but we only need to ask to have our sins forgiven.

The first step toward the soul's recovery is the knowledge of the sin committed.

SENECA

Forgive Others First

"And whenever you stand praying, if you have anything against anyone, forgive him, that your Father in heaven may also forgive you your trespasses."

Mark 11:25 (NKJV)

We can't expect our own sins to be forgiven when we haven't forgiven others. Forgive and then be forgiven.

The noblest vengeance is to forgive.

English Proverb

A Reason For Forgiveness

"I, even I, am he who blots out your transgressions, for my own sake, and remembers your sins no more."

Isaiah 43:25 (NIV)

Have you ever wondered why God wants to forgive you? Because He wants the benefit of your fellowship.

God pardons like a mother, who kisses the offense into everlasting forgiveness.

Henry Ward Beecher

Forgiven Sins

> *. . . as far as the east is from the west, so far*
> *has he removed our transgressions from us.*
>
> PSALMS 103:12 (NIV)

Are you glad God doesn't put your forgiven sins
where the North meets the South? You could find
them there. Your forgiven sins are as far from you
as the nonexistent place of where the East meets
the West.

Sin is sovereign till sovereign grace dethrones it.

CHARLES H. SPURGEON

Abundant Forgiveness

Take away my sin, and I will be clean. Wash me, and I will be whiter than snow.

Psalms 51:7 (NCV)

Feeling distant from God? It only takes a turn in His direction and He is right there with more than enough forgiveness.

One reason sin flourishes is that it is treated like a cream puff instead of a rattlesnake.

Billy Sunday

Never Feel Guilty

In him we have redemption through his blood, the forgiveness of sins, in accordance with the riches of God's grace that he lavished on us with all wisdom and understanding. And he made known to us the mystery of his will according to his good pleasure, which he purposed in Christ,

EPHESIANS 1:7–9 (NIV)

Once you've asked for forgiveness, you need never feel guilty. You're redeemed. You're cleansed. Because of God's rich grace.

Man is born broken. He lives by mending. The grace of God is glue.

EUGENE O'NEILL

No Condemnation

So now, those who are in Christ Jesus are not judged guilty.

ROMANS 8:1 (NCV)

Are you "in Christ?" If so, then you don't need to talk or think negatively about yourself!

Throw your sins into the middle of the sea and put up a sign, "No Fishing."

CORRIE TEN BOOM

Erased Forever

How blessed is he whose transgression is forgiven, Whose sin is covered!

PSALMS 32:1 (NASB)

When God forgives your sin, He makes it disappear as if it were erased off a blackboard.

God has a big eraser.

BILLY ZEOLI

Godly Life

For what the law was powerless to do in that it was weakened by the sinful nature, God did by sending his own Son in the likeness of sinful man to be a sin offering. And so he condemned sin in sinful man, in order that the righteous requirements of the law might be fully met in us, who do not live according to the sinful nature but according to the Spirit.

ROMANS 8:3–4 (NIV)

Godliness results not from gritting our teeth trying to obey, but giving control to the Holy Spirit's power.

The greatest mistake you can make in life is to be continually fearing that you will make one.

ELBERT HUBBARD

Unmeasurable Love

I pray that Christ will live in your hearts by
faith and that your life will be strong in love
and be built on love. And I pray that you and all
God's holy people will have the power to
understand the greatness of Christ's love—how
wide and how long and how high and how deep
that love is. Christ's love is greater than anyone
can ever know, but I pray that you will be able to
know that love. Then you can be filled with the
fullness of God.

EPHESIANS 3:17–19 (NCV)

Have you ever tried to measure God's love? You
can't do it. We can only enjoy it and be filled up
with it; but even more spills out.

Love is the greatest thing that God can give us;
for himself is love: and it is the greatest thing
we can give to God.

JEREMY TAYLOR

God Rejoices Over You

The LORD your God is with you, he is mighty to save. He will take great delight in you, he will quiet you with his love, he will rejoice over you with singing.

Zephaniah 3:17 (NIV)

When was the last time someone sang a happy song because they were glad to see you? Well, God is doing it all the time.

Seek to cultivate a buoyant, joyous sense of the crowded kindnesses of God in your daily life.

Alexander MacLaren

Undeserved Love

But God demonstrates his own love for us in this: While we were still sinners, Christ died for us.

ROMANS 5:8 (NIV)

What a relief that we don't have to earn God's love. It's a free gift revealed through Jesus' sacrifice.

When you have nothing left but God, then for the first time you become aware that God is enough.

MAUDE ROYDEN

Incorruptible Promise

*Now that you have purified yourselves by
obeying the truth so that you have sincere love
for your brothers, love one another deeply, from
the heart.*

1 PETER 1:22 (NIV)

Our salvation will never disintegrate because God's
promises never fail.

An infinite God can give all of Himself to each of
His children. He does not distribute Himself that
each may have a part, but to each one He gives all
of Himself as fully as if there were no others.

A. W. TOZER

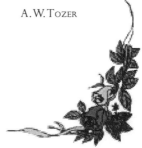

Unseparable Love

Yes, I am sure that neither death, nor life, nor angels, nor ruling spirits, nothing now, nothing in the future, no powers, nothing above us, nothing below us, nor anything else in the whole world will ever be able to separate us from the love of God that is in Christ Jesus our Lord.

ROMANS 8:38–39 (NCV)

Absolutely nothing need separate you from God's love—except your choice to not receive it.

There is no surprise more wonderful than the surprise of being loved; it is God's finger on man's shoulder.

CHARLES MORGAN

Godly Self-Esteem

Therefore, I urge you, brothers, in view of God's mercy, to offer your bodies as living sacrifices, holy and pleasing to God—this is your spiritual act of worship.

ROMANS 12:1 (NIV)

Godly self-esteem is just looking at myself through God's eyes: acknowledging my weaknesses and giving God the credit for my talents.

The Christian who has the smile of God needs no status symbols.

LEONARD RAVENHILL

Promise Of A Loving Father

For you have not received a spirit of slavery
leading to fear again, but you have received a
spirit of adoption as sons by which we cry out,
"Abba! Father!"

ROMANS 8:15 (NASB)

We have been spiritually adopted by the most loving, caring Father possible. Talk about security!

There is no need to plead that the love of God shall fill our heart as though he were unwilling to fill us. He is willing as light is willing to flood a room that is opened to its brightness; willing as water is willing to flow into an emptied channel.

AMY CARMICHAEL

Unrequested Love

This is what real love is: It is not our love for God; it is God's love for us in sending his Son to be the way to take away our sins.

1 JOHN 4:10 (NCV)

What a thrill to know God's love isn't dependent on us loving Him. He can't *not* love us.

God soon turns from his wrath, but he never turns from his love.

CHARLES H. SPURGEON

Abundant Grace And Mercy

*For if ye turn again unto the LORD, your
brethren and your children shall find compassion before them that lead them captive, so that
they shall come again into this land: for the
LORD your God is gracious and merciful, and
will not turn away his face from you, if ye
return unto him.*

2 CHRONICLES 30:9 (KJV)

Feeling hopeless? Mercy is "unlimited second
chances." No matter how many times you need
God's grace and mercy, He offers it to you!

Grace is getting another chance even though you
haven't earned it or deserved it. (You may not even
want it!)

FRITZ RIDENOUR

Perfect Love

There is no fear in love. But perfect love drives out fear, because fear has to do with punishment. The one who fears is not made perfect in love.

1 JOHN 4:18 (NIV)

Are you looking to be loved perfectly? Look no further. Your Heavenly Father loves you in exactly the way you need.

If the Lord be with us, we have no cause of fear. His eye is upon us, His arm over us, His ear open to our prayer—His grace sufficient, His promise unchangeable.

JOHN NEWTON

Long-Suffering Promises

*The Lord is not slow in keeping his promise, as
some understand slowness. He is patient with
you, not wanting anyone to perish, but everyone
to come to repentance.*

2 PETER 3:9 (NIV)

If God isn't taking revenge on your enemies, keep
in mind that you are seeing God's patience in action. He wants them to turn from their evil ways.

The hardness of God is kinder than the softness of
men, and his compulsion is our liberation.

C.S. LEWIS

He Will Complete It!

. . . being confident of this, that he who began
a good work in you will carry it on to comple-
tion until the day of Christ Jesus.

PHILIPPIANS 1:6 (NIV)

If you're thinking God wants you to be perfect on this earth, relax! He'll keep working in you until you see Him in person.

When the divine owner takes possession of a property, he has a twofold objective: intense cultivation and abounding fruitfulness.

NORMAN P. GRUBB

Proven Action

*Declaring the end from the beginning, and from
ancient times the things that are not yet done,
saying, My counsel shall stand, and I will do all
my pleasure: Calling a ravenous bird from the
east, the man that executeth my counsel from a
far country: yea, I have spoken it, I will also bring
it to pass; I have purposed it, I will also do it.*

ISAIAH 46:10–11 (KJV)

Even though it takes longer than we may like at
times, God will bring His plans to fruition. You can
count on it.

Dios tarda pero no olvida—God delays but doesn't
forget.

SPANISH PROVERB

Victory

*But in all these things we overwhelmingly
conquer through Him who loved us.*

ROMANS 8:37 (NASB)

God promises you victory in life because He is
greater than anything difficult you face.

One on God's side is a majority.

WENDELL PHILLIPS

Guarantee Of Deliverance

People who do what is right may have many problems, but the Lord will solve them all.

PSALMS 34:19 (NCV)

While we have no guarantee God will remove or protect us from trials, we can hold onto the guarantee God will walk with us through them until He delivers us.

Afflictions are but the shadow of God's wings.

GEORGE MACDONALD

Abundance

Through these he has given us his very great
and precious promises, so that through them you
may participate in the divine nature and escape
the corruption in the world caused by evil
desires.

2 PETER 1:4 (NIV)

God knows exactly how He wants to use His promises in your life. They are meant to bring great blessings. Look for them!

". . . if you would spend a month feeding on the precious promises of God—you wouldn't be going about complaining how poor you are. You would lift up your head and proclaim the riches of His Grace, because you couldn't help doing it!"

DWIGHT L. MOODY

Living In God's Power

So he said to me, "This is the word of the LORD
to Zerubbabel: 'Not by might nor by power, but
by my Spirit,' says the LORD Almighty."

ZECHARIAH 4:6 (NIV)

Though your own power may seem sufficient to
handle a situation, call upon the Holy Spirit's power
instead.

God commands us to be filled with the Spirit; and
if we aren't filled, it's because we're living beneath
our privileges.

D. L. MOODY

We Are Shielded

As for God, his way is perfect; the word of the LORD is flawless. He is a shield for all who take refuge in him.

PSALMS 18:30 (NIV)

When we are assaulted by life, God puts up His shield to protect us so that we can believe He knows exactly what He's doing to draw us closer to Him.

Do not pray for easy lives. Pray to be stronger men. Do not pray for tasks equal to your powers. Pray for powers equal to your tasks.

PHILLIPS BROOKS

Power In Jesus' Name

You may ask me for anything in my name, and
I will do it.

JOHN 14:14 (NIV)

There is power in Jesus' Name. Praying in Jesus'
Name means you are depending upon Him and not
yourself.

Nothing lies beyond the reach of prayer except that
which lies outside the will of God.

ANONYMOUS

Jesus Will Finish It

Looking unto Jesus the author and finisher of
our faith; who for the joy that was set before him
endured the cross, despising the shame, and is set
down at the right hand of the throne of God.

HEBREWS 12:2 (KJV)

We may think we make our faith grow, but actually it's God's promise that Jesus does it within us— from the inside out—as we cooperate with Him.

We cannot force ourselves to have faith in God. We are as much in need in this respect as in everything else. Faith can only originate in the soul of man by the gift of God.

MARCUS L. LOANE

Praise God

Praise the LORD, O my soul; all my inmost being, praise his holy name. Praise the LORD, O my soul, and forget not all his benefits—who forgives all your sins and heals all your diseases, who redeems your life from the pit and crowns you with love and compassion, who satisfies your desires with good things so that your youth is renewed like the eagle's.

PSALMS 103:1–5 (NIV)

Praising God helps you to remember all the fabulous things He has done for you.

Gratitude is born in hearts that take time to count up past mercies.

CHARLES E. JE`PFFERSON

God Gives From His Abundance

And my God shall supply all your need
according to His riches in glory by Christ Jesus.

PHILIPPIANS 4:19 (NKJV)

God is certainly generous at times in providing for our wants, but without question, He'll always provide for our true needs.

A luxury is something you don't need but can't do without.

ANONYMOUS

Life!

I will never forget your orders, because you have given me life by them.

PSALMS 119:93 (NCV)

We all want quality of life. The ultimate blessed life results from obeying God's rules. They are for our good.

God always gives His best to those who leave the choice with Him.

JIM ELLIOT

God's Arms Are Long!

Behold, the LORD'S hand is not shortened,
that it cannot save; neither his ear heavy, that it
cannot hear:

ISAIAH 59:1 (KJV)

Though we may feel distant from God, be assured
His hands really are holding us up and His ears are
tuned to hear our cries.

God builds the nest of the blind bird.

TURKISH PROVERB

Promise Of Salvation

But anyone who asks for mercy from the Lord shall have it and shall be saved.

ACTS 2:21 (LIVING)

Sometimes we doubt God's desire to establish our friendship with Him, but we don't need to. There are no conditions, other than call on Him!

I am not what I ought to be, I am not what I wish to be, I am not what I hope to be; but, by the grace of God, I am not what I was.

JOHN NEWTON

Guaranteed Triumph

But thanks be to God, who always leads us in triumphal procession in Christ and through us spreads everywhere the fragrance of the knowledge of him.

2 CORINTHIANS 2:14 (NIV)

The battle is already won, we just have to keep obeying the commands of our Commander.

Triumph is just umph added to try.

ANONYMOUS

Assured Help

The righteous cry out, and the LORD hears
them; he delivers them from all their troubles.

Psalms 34:17 (NIV)

You only need to ask and God will be right there to
help you in the midst of pain or struggle.

"O Lord, help me to understand that you ain't goin'
to let nuthin' come my way that You and me together can't handle."

Southern Prayer

No Lack

The Lord is my shepherd; I have everything I need.

PSALMS 23:1 (NCV)

Just as a shepherd leads his sheep to green meadows, Jesus, your Heavenly Shepherd, will make sure anything you truly need is provided.

Nowhere in the Bible does it say that God is going to give you a plan for your entire life. What He does promise is to lead you as you go; to direct you day by day; to show you His will hour by hour.

TONY CAMPOLO

Sufficiency

*And God is able to make all grace abound
toward you; that ye, always having all sufficiency in all things, may abound to every good
work.*

2 CORINTHIANS 9:8 (KJV)

If you've ever doubted whether you'll have enough
time or energy for what God wants you to do, fear
not! He'll supply for His assignments.

If God has called you, don't spend time looking
over your shoulder to see who is following.

ANONYMOUS

Lost Way

Jesus answered, "I am the way, and the truth, and the life. The only way to the Father is through me."

JOHN 14:6 (NCV)

God knows we're lost without Him, so He provided a path back to Him through Jesus.

Man's problem rises from the fact that he has not only lost the way, but he has lost the address.

NICOLAS BARDYAEV

No Lack

Even lions may get weak and hungry, but those
who look to the Lord will have every good thing.

PSALMS 34:10 (NCV)

Looking for God's hand in everything that happens
will focus our vision on all the good He's giving.

God's ways are behind the scenes, but he moves all
the scenes which he is behind.

JOHN NELSON DARBY

Gossip Brings Destruction

Without wood a fire goes out; without gossip a quarrel dies down.

PROVERBS 26:20 (NIV)

God promises good things when we refrain from passing along tasty verbal tidbits—that are untrue.

One reason the dog has so many friends: he wags his tail instead of his tongue.

ANONYMOUS

Gentle Words

A gentle answer turns away wrath, but a harsh word stirs up anger.

PROVERBS 15:1 (NIV)

Gentle words bring great benefits. We may think anger motivates others, but it doesn't. Giving positives does.

Anger: an acid that can do more harm to the vessel in which it is stored than to anything on which it is poured.

ANONYMOUS

Control Your Words

The wise of heart will receive commands, But a babbling fool will be thrown down.

PROVERBS 10:8 (NASB)

Though it may feel good at the time, talking negatively about someone will only bring hurt and destruction.

The scorpion carries his poison in his tail, the slanderer carries his in his tongue.

THOMAS WATSON

Being Loudly Quiet

*We all stumble in many ways. If anyone is
never at fault in what he says, he is a perfect
man, able to keep his whole body in check.*

JAMES 3:2 (NIV)

The hardest part of our body to control is our
tongue, but if we do, God says we're almost perfect!

A wise man is one who thinks twice before saying
nothing.

ANONYMOUS

Gossip Hurts

*If you argue your case with a neighbor, do not
betray another man's confidence, or he who
hears it may shame you and you will never lose
your bad reputation.*

PROVERBS 25:9–10 (NIV)

Although at the time gossip seems satisfying, God
promises that your sin will reap consequences.

The only time people dislike gossip is when you
gossip about them.

WILL ROGERS

Pass Along the Forgiveness

Get rid of all bitterness, rage and anger,
brawling and slander, along with every form of
malice. Be kind and compassionate to one
another, forgiving each other, just as in Christ
God forgave you.

EPHESIANS 4:31–32 (NIV)

Jesus isn't angry at you, and you've done a lot wrong to hurt Him. Why not stop being angry at those who have hurt you? It'll be a load off your back.

Swallowing angry words before you say them is better than having to eat them afterwards.

ANONYMOUS

Hold Your Tongue

When words are many, sin is not absent, but he who holds his tongue is wise.

Proverbs 10:19 (NIV)

Although it's difficult to do, God promises to reveal our wisdom when we control our words.

It often shows a fine command of language to say nothing.

Anonymous

Keep Them Guessing

Even a fool is thought wise if he keeps silent,
and discerning if he holds his tongue.

PROVERBS 17:28 (NIV)

Why spoil a person's good opinion of you? Keep your tongue under control.

At times, it is better to keep your mouth shut and let people wonder if you're a fool than to open it and remove all doubt.

JAMES G. SINCLAIR

Self Examination

Every man's way is right in his own eyes, But the LORD weighs the hearts.

PROVERBS 21:2 (NASB)

It's easy to be deceived about ourselves, but God can see the good and the wrong in us even when we try to hide the truth.

As one grows older, one realizes that the things our enemies find hateful about us are hateful.

MAURIAC

Don't Choose Envy

A sound heart is life to the body, But envy is rottenness to the bones.

PROVERBS 14:30 (NKJV)

Jealousy and envy equally bring strife and discontent.

Envy shooteth at others and woundeth herself.

THOMAS FULLER

True Humility

For through the grace given to me I say to every man among you not to think more highly of himself than he ought to think; but to think so as to have sound judgment, as God has allotted to each a measure of faith.

ROMANS 12:3 (NASB)

Thinking rightly about ourselves will bring God's peace and security.

It is possible to be too big for God to use you but never too small for God to use you.

ANONYMOUS

Blessings Of Humility

When pride comes, then comes disgrace, but
with humility comes wisdom.

PROVERBS 11:2 (NIV)

The hard thing about humility is that as soon as you've achieved it, you've lost it. But it stays around when we just focus on Jesus.

The smallest package we have ever seen is a man wrapped up in himself.

ANONYMOUS

Exaltation At Right Time

Humble yourselves, therefore, under God's mighty hand, that he may lift you up in due time.

1 PETER 5:6 (NIV)

It's no fun to not receive credit for how you serve God, but He promises to exalt you at the right time.

In Christian service the branches that bear the most fruit hang the lowest.

ANONYMOUS

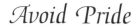

Avoid Pride

The fear of the LORD is the instruction for
wisdom, And before honor comes humility.

PROVERBS 15:33 (NASB)

Everything good we do was orchestrated by God
anyway, so we can give Him the credit, not ourselves.

God hasn't arranged our anatomy so as to make it
easy for us to pat ourselves on the back.

ANONYMOUS

Positive Thinking

Finally, brethren, whatever is true, whatever is
honorable, whatever is right, whatever is pure,
whatever is lovely, whatever is of good repute, if
there is any excellence and if anything worthy
of praise, let your mind dwell on these things.

PHILIPPIANS 4:8 (NASB)

When you're feeling disgruntled and unhappy, just focus on your blessings.

Growl all day and you'll feel dog tired at night.

ANONYMOUS

Comforted From Mourning

Blessed are those who mourn, for they will be comforted.

MATTHEW 5:4 (NIV)

It's hard to believe we can call pain a blessing but once God shows Himself as the God of comfort, we see the benefit.

I saw a star. I reached for it. I missed. So I accepted the sky.

ANONYMOUS

Joyful Heart

*All the days of the oppressed are wretched, but
the cheerful heart has a continual feast.*

PROVERBS 15:15.

Whether each day is wretched or a feast depends
upon your attitude. Choose joy!

"For those who love God, laughter isn't optional,
it's scriptural."

LIZ CURTIS HIGGS.

Rejoice In Each Day

This is the day the LORD has made;We will rejoice and be glad in it.

PSALMS 118:24 (NKJV)

Every single day of your life is planned and created by a God who loves you and wants only good for you.

All created things are living in the Hand of God. The senses see only the action of the creatures; but faith sees in everything the action of God.

J.P. DE CAUSSADE

Choose Joy

The ransomed of the LORD will return. They
will enter Zion with singing; everlasting joy will
crown their heads. Gladness and joy will
overtake them, and sorrow and sighing will flee
away.

ISAIAH 51:11 (NIV)

Happiness is what happens to you, joy is something
you choose. When you choose joy, sadness can't stay
around.

Joy is not happiness so much as gladness; it is the
ecstasy of eternity in a soul that has made peace
with God and is ready to do his will.

ANONYMOUS

Delight In God

Delight yourself in the LORD; And He will
give you the desires of your heart.

PSALMS 37:4 (NASB)

When we delight in God, we are motivated to want
what He wants. Then we can be assured He'll give
us the desires of our hearts.

There are no disappointments to those whose wills
are buried in the will of God.

FREDERICK W. FABER

Hope Replaces Sorrow

But we do not want you to be uninformed,
brethren, about those who are asleep, that you
may not grieve, as do the rest who have no hope.

1 THESSALONIANS 4:13 (NASB)

When we're grieving over the loss of a loved one,
our expectation of seeing them again will replace
some of our sorrow with joy.

Those who love God never meet for the last time.

W.G. ELMSLIE

Absurdly Happy

"These things I have spoken to you, that My joy may be in you, and that your joy may be made full."

JOHN 15:11 (NASB)

Being a Christian doesn't mean having everything go well, but it does mean we can have joy in the midst of whatever happens.

Jesus promised his disciples three things: that they would be completely fearless, absurdly happy, and in constant trouble.

F.R. MALTBY

End Result Of Joy

*Dear friends, do not be surprised at the painful
trial you are suffering, as though something
strange were happening to you.*

*But rejoice that you participate in the sufferings
of Christ, so that you may be overjoyed when his
glory is revealed.*

1 PETER 4:12–13 (NIV)

Though it seems impossible now, you will one day
be joyful about facing trials.

God will not permit any troubles to come upon us,
unless He has a specific plan by which great blessing can come out of the difficulty.

PETER MARSHALL

Joy In The Morning

His anger lasts only a moment, but his kindness
lasts for a lifetime. Crying may last for a night,
but joy comes in the morning.

PSALMS 30:5 (NCV)

It may seem too difficult to go on, but hold on!
Morning's joy will soon dispel the darkness.

The soul would have no rainbow had the eyes no
tears.

JOHN VANCE CHENEY

Mourning Joy

To console those who mourn in Zion, To give them beauty for ashes, The oil of joy for mourning, The garment of praise for the spirit of heaviness; That they may be called trees of righteousness, The planting of the LORD, that He may be glorified."

ISAIAH 61:3 (NKJV)

As we weather difficulties that bring great pain, God will be glorified as others see we are strong in Him.

The brook would lose its song if we removed the rocks.

ANONYMOUS

Unrestricted Love

*"Love the Lord your God with all your heart
and with all your soul and with all your mind
and with all your strength. The second is this:
'Love your neighbor as yourself.' There is no
commandment greater than these."*

MARK 12:30–31 (NIV)

When we love God, that love will be enlarged to
include ourselves and others.

Love doesn't just sit there, like a stone, it has to be
made, like bread; re-made all the time, made new.

URSULA K. LEGUIN

Revealed Love

"Whoever has my commands and obeys them, he is the one who loves me. He who loves me will be loved by my Father, and I too will love him and show myself to him."

JOHN 14:21 (NIV)

The more we know God's love, the more we'll obey Him. The more we obey Him, the more we'll see of God's work in our lives.

When I have learnt to love God better than my earthly dearest, I shall love my earthly dearest better than I do now.

C.S. LEWIS

Undemanding Love

We love because he first loved us.

1 JOHN 4:19 (NIV)

How can we not love God back when He has showed us such an undemanding love?

To believe in God is to love him.

MIGUEL DE UNAMUNO

Love Through Action

In the same way, let your light shine before men, that they may see your good deeds and praise your Father in heaven.

MATTHEW 5:16 (NIV)

We may think giving advice is helpful, but God wants us to really help in action.

What a big difference there is between giving advice and lending a hand.

WATERLOO

Forbearance For Others

Bear with each other and forgive whatever
grievances you may have against one another.
Forgive as the Lord forgave you.

COLOSSIANS 3:13 (NIV)

Compassion and understanding is created by re-
membering how much we each have been forgiven.

A Christian will find it cheaper to pardon than to
resent. Forgiveness saves the expense of anger, the
cost of hatred, the waste of spirits.

HANNAH MORE

Love, Don't Hate

*God is not unjust; he will not forget your work
and the love you have shown him as you have
helped his people and continue to help them.*

HEBREWS 6:10 (NIV)

We may think disliking people will bring satisfaction, but it doesn't. God says He'll reward us for loving others in His Name.

Hating people is like burning down your own house to get rid of a rat.

HARRY EMERSON FOSDICK

Results Of Marital Love

However, each one of you also must love his wife as he loves himself, and the wife must respect her husband.

EPHESIANS 5:33 (NIV)

If we follow God's rules for marriage, each husband will feel respected and each wife will feel loved.

Try praising your wife, even if it frightens her at first.

BILLY SUNDAY

Oneness in Marriage

For this reason a man will leave his father and mother and be united to his wife, and they will become one flesh.

GENESIS 2:24.

If husbands and wives want real unity, they must forsake making their parents their first priority. God wants their spouse to be their primary focus.

"By all means marry. If you get a good wife, you will become very happy; if you get a bad one, you will become a philosopher—and that is good for any man."

SOCRATES.

Blessings Of Obedience

All these blessings will come upon you and accompany you if you obey the LORD your God: You will be blessed in the city and blessed in the country.

DEUTERONOMY 28:2–3 (NIV)

Do you want abundant blessings? That will only happen when you obey God's directions.

Sin is not hurtful because it is forbidden, but sin is forbidden because it is hurtful.

BENJAMIN FRANKLIN

Conformed Or Transformed

Do not change yourselves to be like the people of this world, but be changed within by a new way of thinking. Then you will be able to decide what God wants for you; you will know what is good and pleasing to him and what is perfect.

ROMANS 12:2 (NCV)

Either way, we'll be formed into an image. Either conformed into society's distorted image or transformed to the higher image of Jesus, living out God's will.

It may be true that there are two sides to every question, but it is also true that there are two sides to a sheet of flypaper, and it makes a big difference to the fly which side he chooses.

CHRISTIAN MEDICAL SOCIETY JOURNAL

Good Works Already Planned

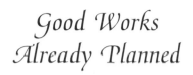

For we are God's workmanship, created in
Christ Jesus to do good works, which God
prepared in advance for us to do.

EPHESIANS 2:10 (NIV)

God can't wait to use you for His glory! In fact,
He's already made His plan.

God chose me because I was weak enough. God
does not do his great works by large committees.
He trains somebody to be quiet enough, and little
enough, and then uses him.

HUDSON TAYLOR

Mustard Seed Sized Faith

And Jesus said unto them, "Because of your unbelief: for verily I say unto you, If ye have faith as a grain of mustard seed, ye shall say unto this mountain, Remove hence to yonder place; and it shall remove; and nothing shall be impossible unto you."

MATTHEW 17:20 (KJV)

Obeying God makes the most amazing things happen—things that are beyond our ability to cause to happen. Therefore, we know it must be God working through us.

A pessimist is one who makes difficulties of his opportunities; an optimist is one who makes opportunities of his difficulties.

REGINALD B. MANSELL

Sowing And Reaping

Do not be deceived, God is not mocked; for
whatever a man sows, that he will also reap.

GALATIANS 6:7 (NKJV)

We may think we can get away with unwise choices,
but God will discipline us for our good.

A man is what he thinks about all day long.

RALPH WALDO EMERSON

Righteous Living

"Then I will give them one heart, and I will put a new spirit within them, and take the stony heart out of their flesh, and give them a heart of flesh, that they may walk in My statutes and keep My judgments and do them; and they shall be My people, and I will be their God."

EZEKIEL 11:19–20 (NKJV)

God wants us to live in a way that glorifies His name. Doing so will help us know we are His child.

So live that you wouldn't be ashamed to sell the family parrot to the town gossip.

ANONYMOUS

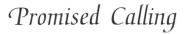

Promised Calling

The one who calls you is faithful and he will do it.

1 Thessalonians 5:24 (NIV)

Has God called you to some purpose or task yet He seems to delay in fulfilling it? Don't be concerned. He will keep His promise.

God's promises are like the stars; the darker the night the brighter they shine.

David Nicholas

Patience Is Smart

*He who is slow to wrath has great understand-
ing, But he who is impulsive exalts folly.*

PROVERBS 14:29 (NKJV)

Anger never really brings the good results we want.

People who fly into a rage always make a bad land-
ing.

WILL ROGERS

Results Belong To God

Now He who supplies seed to the sower and
bread for food, will supply and multiply your
seed for sowing and increase the harvest of your
righteousness.

2 CORINTHIANS 9:10 (NASB)

It's up to God to determine the results of the seeds
He plants in our lives. Don't try to grow a flower if
He wants to grow a tree.

What have we to expect? Anything. What have we
to hope for? Everything. What have we to fear?
Nothing.

EDWARD B. PUSEY

Wait On God

Wait for the LORD; Be strong, and let your
heart take courage; Yes, wait for the LORD.

PSALMS 27:14 (NASB)

It can take time, but God will come through with strength. Look for it.

We must wait for God, long, meekly, in the wind and wet, in the thunder and lightning, in the cold and the dark. Wait, and he will come. He never comes to those who do not wait.

FREDERICK W. FABER

Get Over It!

Be angry but do not sin; do not let the sun go down on your anger, and do not make room for the devil.

EPHESIANS 4:26–27 (NRSV)

Staying angry doesn't make us justified, it just opens a door of opportunity for Satan.

An angry man is again angry with himself when he returns to reason.

PUBLICIUS SYRUS

Supernatural Peace

And the peace of God, which transcends all
understanding, will guard your hearts and your
minds in Christ Jesus.

PHILIPPIANS 4:7 (NIV)

No one can explain it, but God's supernatural peace
invades your heart when you surrender your cares
to Him.

The capital of heaven is the heart in which Jesus
Christ is enthroned as King.

SADHU SUNDAR SINGH

Peace With Almighty God

Therefore, since we have been justified through faith, we have peace with God through our Lord Jesus Christ.

ROMANS 5:1 (NIV)

It's incredible but we can have a friendship with a holy God who demands perfection because we wrap ourselves in Jesus' robe of righteousness.

Oh what a pearl of great price is the lowest degree of the peace of God.

JOHN WESLEY

Choose Peace

*Peace I leave with you; my peace I give you. I do
not give to you as the world gives. Do not let
your hearts be troubled and do not be afraid.*

JOHN 14:27 (NIV)

There are a plethora of things that can create fear
and confusion. But focusing on Jesus' promise of
peace can dissolve fear's hold.

How can you expect God to speak in that gentle
and inward voice which melts the soul, when you
are making so much noise with your rapid reflec-
tions? Be silent and God will speak again.

FRANCOIS FENELON

Wait For The Reaping

And let us not be weary in well doing: for in
due season we shall reap, if we faint not.

GALATIANS 6:9 (KJV)

The harvest seems like a long time away, but if you'll persevere, you'll see the fruit of your efforts.

Even the woodpecker owes his success to the fact that he uses his head and keeps pecking away until he finishes the job he starts.

COLEMAN COX

Need Of Endurance

Therefore do not cast away your confidence, which has great reward. For you have need of endurance, so that after you have done the will of God, you may receive the promise.

HEBREWS 10:35–36 (NKJV)

If you're feeling weary in doing God's will, hold on to God's promises. They will sustain you.

It is more important to gird ourselves for the grind of life than it is to throw ourselves into high gear only for the grandiose affairs of life.

CHARLES CALDWELL RYRIE

Down But Not Out

We are afflicted in every way, but not crushed;
perplexed, but not driven to despair; persecuted,
but not forsaken; struck down, but not destroyed;
always carrying in the body the death of Jesus,
so that the life of Jesus may also be made visible
in our bodies.

2 CORINTHIANS 4:8–10 (NRSV)

No matter how discouraged or mistreated you are, knowing how much Jesus suffered for you will sustain you.

It is impossible for that man to despair who remembers that his helper is omnipotent.

JEREMY TAYLOR

Results Of Testing

In this you greatly rejoice, though now for a little while you may have had to suffer grief in all kinds of trials. These have come so that your faith—of greater worth than gold, which perishes even though refined by fire—may be proved genuine and may result in praise, glory and honor when Jesus Christ is revealed.

1 PETER 1:6–7 (NIV)

When we're in the pits of trials, it's hard to see the diamonds buried in the mud. But staying firm will wash away the mud and reveal the sparkles.

Great works are performed not by strength but by perseverance.

SAMUEL JOHNSON

God Is Faithful

*Let us hold fast the confession of our hope
without wavering, for He who promised is
faithful.*

HEBREWS 10:23 (NKJV)

We can stay strong in our faith, not because we are
faithful but because He is.

Christ is greater than our faith in him.

JAMES HASTINGS

Private Prayer

But whenever you pray, go into your room and
shut the door and pray to your Father who is in
secret; and your Father who sees in secret will
reward you.

Matthew 6:6 (NRSV)

The most exciting thing about prayer is that it can
be done in the quiet of the heart—and God hears!

A man who prays much in private will make short
prayers in public.

D. L. Moody

Unexpected Answer

"Call to me and I will answer you and tell you great and unsearchable things you do not know."

JEREMIAH 33:3 (NIV)

Be sure to call to God, but don't be surprised if He gives you an unexpected answer. He knows best.

Keep praying, but be thankful that God's answers are wiser than your prayers!

WILLIAM CULBERTSON

Powerful Prayer

"Again, I tell you that if two of you on earth agree about anything you ask for, it will be done for you by my Father in heaven."

Matthew 18:19 (NIV)

Gathering with others for prayer brings great results for God's kingdom. ·

The only footprints on the sands of time, that will really last, are the ones made after knee-prints!

C. W. Renwick

Answers To Prayer

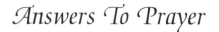

And this is the confidence that we have in him,
that, if we ask any thing according to his will,
he heareth us: And if we know that he hear us,
whatsoever we ask, we know that we have the
petitions that we desired of him.

1 JOHN 5:14–15 (KJV)

If you are seeking God's heart, you will know His will and have your prayers answered.

The man or woman who is wholly or joyously surrendered to Christ can't make a wrong choice— any choice will be the right one.

A. W. TOZER

Bold Entrance

Let us therefore come boldly to the throne of grace, that we may obtain mercy and find grace to help in time of need.

HEBREWS 4:16 (NKJV)

God promises to let us in when we boldly knock at the door of His throne room. How like His mercy and grace!

Groanings which cannot be uttered are often prayers which cannot be refused.

C.H. SPURGEON

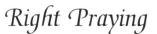

Right Praying

Therefore I tell you, whatever you ask for in prayer, believe that you have received it, and it will be yours.

Mark 11:24 (NIV)

If you've prayed according to God's will, you don't have to doubt at all that God will answer you.

Prayer is not overcoming God's reluctance; it is laying hold of his highest willingness.

Richard Chenevix Trench

Seek The Good Things

"And do not seek what you shall eat, and what you shall drink, and do not keep worrying. For all these things the nations of the world eagerly seek; but your Father knows that you need these things. But seek for His kingdom, and these things shall be added to you."

LUKE 12:29–31 (NASB)

Isn't it a relief that we don't have to let our basic needs overshadow our relationship with God? The Lord God Almighty promises to provide everything we truly need.

The faith of Christ offers no buttons to push for quick service. The new order must wait the Lord's own time, and that is too much for the man in a hurry.

A. W. TOZER

Crucified Life

*I have been crucified with Christ and I no
longer live, but Christ lives in me. The life I live
in the body, I live by faith in the Son of God,
who loved me and gave himself for me.*

GALATIANS 2:20 (NIV)

It's a paradox and a promise of God that dying to self brings life. Real life! Abundant life!

Never put a question mark where God has put a period.

JOHN R. RICE

Concentrate On Today

The fear of man brings a snare, But he who trusts in the LORD will be exalted.

We only have today. Spend it wisely.

Yesterday is a canceled check, tomorrow is a promissory note, but today is cash in hand.

ANONYMOUS

Through Life Or Death

For whether we live, we live unto the Lord; and
whether we die, we die unto the Lord: whether
we live therefore, or die, we are the Lord's.

ROMANS 14:8 (KJV)

We're either living on earth or living in heaven.
Either way, we win!

Death is not a period but a comma in the story of
life.

AMOS J. TARVER

Why Worry?

Do not boast about tomorrow, for you do not
know what a day may bring forth.

PROVERBS 27:1 (NIV)

Focusing on yesterday or tomorrow only brings discontentment. Focus on today.

You cannot buy yesterday back with the tears or prayers or votive offerings of today.

CLARENCE EDWARD MACARTNEY

Make Christ The Priority

*Since, then, you have been raised with Christ, set
your hearts on things above, where Christ is
seated at the right hand of God.*

COLOSSIANS 3:1 (NIV)

It takes a choice, but we can make Jesus our highest
priority.

Christ is not valued at all unless he is valued above all.

AUGUSTINE

Value Christ

What is more, I consider everything a loss
compared to the surpassing greatness of knowing
Christ Jesus my Lord, for whose sake I have lost all
things. I consider them rubbish, that I may gain
Christ and be found in him, not having a righ-
teousness of my own that comes from the law, but
that which is through faith in Christ—the
righteousness that comes from God and is by faith.
                                    PHILIPPIANS 3:8–9 (NIV)

Valuing Christ over everything else doesn't subtract
from your life—it enhances it—with God's promise of being acceptable to Him.

Thou hast made us for Thyself, and the heart of
man is restless until it finds its rest in Thee.

                                    SAINT AUGUSTINE

Set Priorities

Consider my affliction and deliver me, For I do not forget Your law.

Plead my cause and redeem me; Revive me according to Your word.

Psalms 119:153–154 (NKJV)

When you set God's ideas high on your priorities, God will come through for you.

One thorn of experience is worth a whole wilderness of warning.

James Russell Lowell

Turning Away From The Worthless

Turn my heart toward your statutes and not toward selfish gain. Turn my eyes away from worthless things; preserve my life according to your word.

PSALMS 119:37 (NIV)

When we are reminded through God's Word of His abundant provision, we will be eager to take our eyes off the things others have.

Read the Bible. Free gift inside.

ANONYMOUS

True Satisfaction

Better is a dish of vegetables where love is, Than a fattened ox and hatred with it.

PROVERBS 15:17 (NASB)

You may think money will make you happy, but love is of higher gain.

Money will buy a fine dog, but only love will make him wag his tail.

ANONYMOUS

Fear Of Man

So we can be sure when we say, "I will not be afraid, because the Lord is my helper. People can't do anything to me."

HEBREWS 13:6 (NCV)

Needing people's approval can fuel fear. Don't worry about them! Only about pleasing God.

We need to learn to set our course by the stars and not by the lights of every passing ship.

OMAR BRADLEY

Representing God

*He lifted me out of the slimy pit, out of the mud
and mire; he set my feet on a rock and gave me a
firm place to stand. He put a new song in my
mouth, a hymn of praise to our God. Many will
see and fear and put their trust in the LORD.
Blessed is the man who makes the LORD his
trust, who does not look to the proud, to those
who turn aside to false gods.*

PSALMS 40:2–4 (NIV)

When you give God the credit for His work in your
life, He'll cause other people to acknowledge Him
too.

No pain, no palm; no thorns, no throne; no gall, no
glory; no cross, no crown.

WILLIAM PENN

Priorities Produce Peace

"Therefore I tell you, do not worry about your life, what you will eat or drink; or about your body, what you will wear. Is not life more important than food, and the body more important than clothes? Look at the birds of the air; they do not sow or reap or store away in barns, and yet your heavenly Father feeds them. Are you not much more valuable than they?"

MATTHEW 6:25–26 (NIV)

Wanting the wrong things brings chaos. But wanting God's will brings complete fulfillment.

Some of us do not believe we are having a good time unless we are doing something we can't afford.

ANONYMOUS

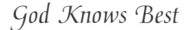

God Knows Best

For my thoughts are not your thoughts, neither
are your ways my ways, saith the LORD. For as
the heavens are higher than the earth, so are my
ways higher than your ways, and my thoughts
than your thoughts.

ISAIAH 55:8–9 (KJV)

God sees everything from a much better perspective. He has the better plan.

Live near to God, and all things will appear little to you in comparison with eternal realities.

ROBERT MURRAY MCCHEYNE

Secure in Christ

David said about him:"I saw the Lord always before me. Because he is at my right hand, I will not be shaken."

Acts 2:25 (NIV)

When we have a sense of Jesus' presence, we don't have to let life's bumps make us feel insecure. We are rooted into a firm foundation.

Faith makes a Christian. Life proves a Christian. Trial confirms a Christian. Death crowns a Christian.

Anonymous

Spiritual Food

Jesus answered, "It is written: 'Man does not live on bread alone, but on every word that comes from the mouth of God.'"

MATTHEW 4:4 (NIV)

Of course, we need to eat food to nourish our bodies, but it's much more important to feed our souls.

First I shake the whole [apple] tree, that the ripest might fall. Then I climb the tree and shake each limb, and then each branch and then each twig, and then I look under each leaf.

MARTIN LUTHER

Power Living

For God did not give us a spirit of timidity, but
a spirit of power, of love and of self-discipline.

2 TIMOTHY 1:7 (NIV)

God does not want us to ever fear. Instead, He promises to supply the insight, strength and ability to respond as we need it in each circumstance—at the time we need it, and usually not before.

I don't claim anything of the work. It is his work. I am like a little pencil in his hand. That is all. He does the thinking. He does the writing. The pencil has nothing to do with it. The pencil has only to be allowed to be used.

MOTHER TERESA

Declared Innocent!

My little children, I am writing these things to you so that you may not sin. But if anyone does sin, we have an advocate with the Father, Jesus Christ the righteous.

1 JOHN 2:1 (NRSV)

Wouldn't you love to be represented in court by the best lawyer in the world? Jesus represents you in the court of heaven and He always wins His case.

If I could hear Christ praying for me in the next room, I would not fear a million enemies. Yet distance makes no difference. He is praying for me.

ROBERT MURRAY MCCHEYNE

Purposeful Comfort

Now may our Lord Jesus Christ himself and
God our Father, who loved us and through
grace gave us eternal comfort and good hope,
comfort your hearts and strengthen them in
every good work and word.

2 THESSALONIANS 2:16–17 (NRSV)

Sadness often obscures our ability to see God's work
through us. But God promises to open our eyes as
to how He's using us even during hard times.

It is easier to suffer in silence if you are sure someone is watching.

WARREN

Sufficient Grace

But he said to me, "My grace is sufficient for you, for my power is made perfect in weakness." Therefore I will boast all the more gladly about my weaknesses, so that Christ's power may rest on me.

2 CORINTHIANS 12:9 (NIV)

If you're feeling weak today, rejoice! As you cooperate with the Lord, His strength will enlarge to fit your need.

Weak things united become strong.

THOMAS FULLER

Protection

When you pass through the waters, I will be
with you; and when you pass through the rivers,
they will not sweep over you. When you walk
through the fire, you will not be burned; the
flames will not set you ablaze.

ISAIAH 43:2 (NIV)

Even though you encounter very difficult problems,
God promises to walk through them with you.

A Christian is like a teabag—he's not worth much
until he's been through some hot water.

ANONYMOUS

Hope Breeds Courage

Be of good courage, and he shall strengthen
your heart, all ye that hope in the LORD.

PSALMS 31:24 (KJV)

If we believe God is in control of us and our cir-
cumstances, that's hope. Hope put into action is
courage: the ability to obey God regardless of the
cost.

I would rather walk with God in the dark than go
alone in the light.

MARY GARDINER BRAINARD

Strength In Jesus

I can do everything through him who gives me strength.

PHILIPPIANS 4:13 (NIV)

For whatever you face, God promises to supply the needed strength. You only need to ask.

Jesus Christ didn't come into my heart to sit down; he started moving around.

ANDY HAMILTON

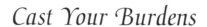

Cast Your Burdens

Cast your cares on the LORD and he will
sustain you; he will never let the righteous fall.

PSALMS 55:22 (NIV)

Are you weighed down with burdens? Lift them
onto Jesus' capable shoulders.

A Christian should never let adversity get him down
except on his knees.

MAE NICHOLSON

Be Strong!

Be strong and courageous, do not be afraid or
tremble at them, for the LORD your God is the
one who goes with you. He will not fail you or
forsake you.

DEUTERONOMY 31:6 (NASB)

God is always with you, therefore you can fight off
feelings of fear.

The adventurous life is not one exempt from fear,
but on the contrary one that is lived in full knowledge of fears of all kinds, one in which we go for-
ward in spite of our fears.

PAUL TOURNIER

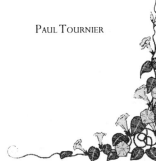

Wings Like Eagles

. . . but those who hope in the LORD will renew their strength. They will soar on wings like eagles; they will run and not grow weary, they will walk and not be faint.

ISAIAH 40:31 (NIV)

God wants you to persevere. If you're feeling weak, take hold of His offer of eagles' wings and soar!

"They that wait upon the Lord shall renew their strength." They that wait upon men often dissipate their energies.

LEONARD RAVENHILL

Let Go

Casting all your care upon him; for he careth for you.

1 Peter 5:7 (KJV)

Because God wants only the best for you, you can hand your problems and frustrations over to His capable hands.

The highest pinnacle of the spiritual life is not joy in unbroken sunshine, but absolute and undoubting trust in the love of God.

A. W. Thorold

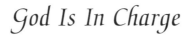

God Is In Charge

"Let not your heart be troubled; you believe in God, believe also in Me."

JOHN 14:1 (NKJV)

If you know God is in charge of your life, your heart won't be troubled.

If God sends us stony paths, he provides strong shoes.

CORRIE TEN BOOM

Sutures For A Broken Heart

He heals the brokenhearted and bandages their wounds.

PSALMS 147:3 (NCV)

For each wounded heart, God knows the unique and individualized surgery He will heal it with.

The world breaks everyone and afterwards many are strong at the broken places.

ERNEST HEMINGWAY

No More Death

Where, O death, is your victory? Where, O death,
is your sting?

1 CORINTHIANS 15:55 (NIV)

Although loss through death is always painful, death
doesn't have the final word. God does.

If it weren't for death, life would be unbearable.

MALCOLM MUGGERIDGE

Look Up

The Lord says, "I will make my people strong with power from me! They will go wherever they wish, and wherever they go they will be under my personal care."

ZECHARIAH 10:12 (LIVING)

God will be faithful to help us, not because we deserve it, but because He's faithful.

One advantage of being thrown on your back is that you face heaven.

BISHOP FULTON SHEEN

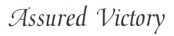

Assured Victory

You are of God, little children, and have
overcome them, because He who is in you is
greater than he who is in the world.

1 JOHN 4:4 (NKJV)

Even though it seems like evil forces are winning
on this earth, God will have the final victory because He's so much stronger—and He wrote the
script!

God has never lost a game and has never tied one.

BILL KRISHER

Strong Tower

The name of the LORD is a strong tower; the
righteous run to it and are safe.

PROVERBS 18:10 (NIV)

Run toward God, not away. He wants to be there
for you.

It is not the will of God to give us more troubles
than will bring us to live by faith in him.

WILLIAM ROMAINE

You're Not Alone

*What, then, shall we say in response to this? If
God is for us, who can be against us?*

ROMANS 8:31 (NIV)

No matter how alone or misunderstood you feel,
Jesus understands. He's rooting for your success in
His power.

Christ's cross is such a burden as sails are to a ship
or wings to a bird.

SAMUEL RUTHERFORD

The Lord's Joy Is Strength

Nehemiah said, "Go and enjoy choice food and sweet drinks, and send some to those who have nothing prepared. This day is sacred to our Lord. Do not grieve, for the joy of the LORD is your strength."

NEHEMIAH 8:10 (NIV)

Do you need strength today? It's available through the joy of knowing the Lord God Almighty is in charge of your life.

Joy is the standard that flies on the battlements of the heart when the King is in residence.

R. LEONARD SMALL

Increased Strength

He gives power to the weak, And to those who have no might He increases strength.

ISAIAH 40:29 (NKJV)

When you're at the end of your rope, God delights in grabbing your hand and pulling you up.

Courage is fear that has said its prayers.

KARLE WILSON BAKER

Sacrifice Brings Blessings

*And everyone who has left houses or brothers or
sisters or father or mother or children or fields
for my sake will receive a hundred times as
much and will inherit eternal life. But many
who are first will be last, and many who are last
will be first.*

MATTHEW 19:29–30 (NIV)

It's no fun to be misunderstood because of a com-
mitment to Christ, but Jesus promises to bless you
for it.

Character cannot be developed in ease and quiet.
Only through experience of trial and suffering can
the soul be strengthened, vision cleared, ambition
inspired, and success achieved.

HELEN KELLER

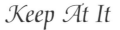

Keep At It

So my dear brothers and sisters, stand strong.
Do not let anything change you. Always give
yourselves fully to the work of the Lord, because
you know that your work in the Lord is never
wasted.

1 CORINTHIANS 15:58 (NCV)

Although serving God gets wearying at times, don't
give up! Persevere! God's rewards are waiting!

By perseverance the snail reached the Ark.

SPURGEON

Needless Fear

So do not fear, for I am with you; do not be dismayed, for I am your God. I will strengthen you and help you; I will uphold you with my righteous right hand.

ISAIAH 41:10 (NIV)

There's no need to be afraid because God promises to embolden you with His strong right hand.

Faith never knows where it is being led, but it loves and knows the One who is leading.

OSWALD CHAMBERS

Strength for Stress

For the eyes of the LORD run to and fro throughout the whole earth, to show Himself strong on behalf of those whose heart is loyal to Him.

2 CHRONICLES 16:9 (NKJV)

When you're feeling undone by stress, know God is watching and will bring the strength you need to fulfill His plan.

You cannot play the fiddle with a loose string.

VANCE HAVNER

Enjoy Your Work

The sluggard craves and gets nothing, but the desires of the diligent are fully satisfied.

PROVERBS 13:4 (NIV)

Whatever God has given you to do, enjoy it! It's His provision for you.

It is not in doing what you like, but in liking what you do that is the secret of happiness.

JAMES BARRIE

Source Of Prosperity

Early in the morning they left for the Desert of
Tekoa. As they set out, Jehoshaphat stood and
said, "Listen to me, Judah and people of Jerusa-
lem! Have faith in the LORD your God and you
will be upheld; have faith in his prophets and
you will be successful."

2 CHRONICLES 20:20 (NIV)

Do you want to be successful? Then believe God
and obey what He says.

Throughout the Bible . . . when God asked a man
to do something, methods, means, materials and
specific directions were always provided. The man
had one thing to do: obey.

ELISABETH ELLIOT

Escape For Temptation

The only temptation that has come to you is that which everyone has. But you can trust God, who will not permit you to be tempted more than you can stand. But when you are tempted, he will also give you a way to escape so that you will be able to stand it.

1 Corinthians 10:13 (NCV)

If you're being tempted, and it seems there's no way out, keep looking for the window of escape. God is about to open it.

The temptation once yielded to gains power. The crack in the embankment which lets a drop or two ooze through is soon a hole which lets out a flood.

Alexander MacLaren

Flee Temptation

When tempted, no one should say, "God is tempting me." For God cannot be tempted by evil, nor does he tempt anyone; but each one is tempted when, by his own evil desire, he is dragged away and enticed. Then, after desire has conceived, it gives birth to sin; and sin, when it is full-grown, gives birth to death.

JAMES 1:13–15 (NIV)

Don't think God is the source of temptation. He does test us to show us where we're lacking, but He never wants us to fail.

When you flee temptation, leave no forwarding address.

ANONYMOUS

Trapped By Dishonesty

Doing right brings freedom to honest people,
but those who are not trustworthy will be
caught by their own desires.

PROVERBS 11:6 (NCV)

It's a real temptation to tell that little white lie, but only speaking truth gives peace of mind.

Falsehoods not only disagree with truths, but usually quarrel among themselves.

WEBSTER

Let God Take Revenge

Do not take revenge, my friends, but leave room for God's wrath, for it is written:"It is mine to avenge; I will repay," says the Lord.

ROMANS 12:19 (NIV)

It's human nature to want revenge, but God can do it so much better.

A good thing to remember is that you can't save face if you lose your head!

ANONYMOUS

Learn Well

It was good for me to be afflicted so that I might learn your decrees.

PSALMS 119:71 (NIV)

It's no fun, but you will learn the most from the difficulties you face.

He who neglects to drink of the spring of experience is apt to die of thirst in the desert of ignorance.

LING PO

Satan Must Flee!

Submit yourselves, then, to God. Resist the devil, and he will flee from you.

JAMES 4:7 (NIV)

Is your soul's enemy bothering you? Don't let him get you down. Just tell him to leave you alone through Jesus' mighty Name. He must flee.

He that labors is tempted by one devil; he that is idle, by a thousand.

ITALIAN PROVERB

Power For Temptation

How can a young man keep his way pure? By living according to your word.

PSALMS 119:9 (NIV)

If we want strength to live a godly life, we must follow God's directions in the Bible.

It is easier to suppress the first desire than to satisfy all that follow it.

BENJAMIN FRANKLIN

Don't Be Pulled Down

Blessed is the man who does not walk in the counsel of the wicked or stand in the way of sinners or sit in the seat of mockers. But his delight is in the law of the LORD, and on his law he meditates day and night. He is like a tree planted by streams of water, which yields its fruit in season and whose leaf does not wither. whatever he does prospers.

PSALMS 1:1–3 (NIV)

Refusing to be pulled down into sin makes us as secure as a tree's roots drawing nourishment from deep in the earth. No wind of adversity will push it—or us—over.

Collapse in the Christian life is seldom a blowout; it is usually a slow leak.

PAUL E. LITTLE

Jesus Knows!

For we do not have a high priest who is unable to sympathize with our weaknesses, but we have one who has been tempted in every way, just as we are—yet was without sin.

HEBREWS 4:15 (NIV)

Jesus knows what it's like to be tempted. He understands what we're going through and promises to give us strength.

The little birds of the field have God for their caterer.

CERVANTES

Powerful Word Of God

So shall my word be that goeth forth out of my
mouth: it shall not return unto me void, but it
shall accomplish that which I please, and it
shall prosper in the thing whereto I sent it.

ISAIAH 55:11 (KJV)

God's Word always accomplishes His intentions. If someone spiritually digests them, they will be changed.

If a man's Bible is coming apart, it is an indication that he himself is fairly well put together.

JAMES E. JENNINGS

Source Of Wisdom

Since you were a child you have known the
Holy Scriptures which are able to make you
wise. And that wisdom leads to salvation
through faith in Christ Jesus.

2 TIMOTHY 3:15 (NCV)

If you want to be great in faith and wisdom, able to
claim God's promises, it's essential—it's manda-
tory—that you study the Word of God.

It ain't those parts of the Bible that I can't understand
that bother me, it is the parts that I do understand.

MARK TWAIN

Delight In God's Word

Direct me in the path of your commands, for there I find delight.

PSALMS 119:35–36 (NIV)

When we are intimately acquainted with God through the Bible, we will be excited and satisfied about doing what God wants.

A readiness to believe every promise implicitly, to obey every command unhesitatingly, to stand perfect and complete in all the will of God, is the only true spirit of Bible study.

ANDREW MURRAY

Don't Add A Word

*Every word of God is pure; He is a shield to
those who put their trust in Him. Do not add to
His words, Lest He rebuke you, and you be found
a liar.*

PROVERBS 30:5–6 (NKJV)

If we are convicted by God's Word, we may want
to change His message. But don't. Only His un-
changed words will protect you from making wrong
choices.

The Bible will keep you from sin, or sin will keep
you from the Bible.

D.L. MOODY

God Will Give Hope

For whatever was written in earlier times was
written for our instruction, that through
perseverance and the encouragement of the
Scriptures we might have hope.

ROMANS 15:4 (NASB)

History is filled with the fulfillment of God's promises, and it's recorded for us in the Bible.

Swim through your temptations and troubles. Run to the promises; they be our Lord's branches hanging over the water so that his half-drowned children may take a grip of them. Let go that grip and you sink to the bottom.

SAMUEL RUTHERFORD

Fruit From The Word

This book of the law shall not depart from
your mouth, but you shall meditate on it day
and night, so that you may be careful to do
according to all that is written in it; for then
you will make your way prosperous, and then
you will have success.

JOSHUA 1:8 (NASB)

Meditating and obeying the Bible reaps God's promises of security and well-being.

Warning: This Book is habit-forming. Regular use
causes loss of anxiety, decreased appetite for lying,
cheating, stealing, hating. Symptoms: increased sen-
sations of love, peace, joy, compassion.

ANONYMOUS

The Examined Life

For the word of God is living and active and sharper than any two-edged sword, and piercing as far as the division of soul and spirit, of both joints and marrow, and able to judge the thoughts and intentions of the heart.

HEBREWS 4:12 (NASB)

If you want to evaluate yourself, look no further than the Bible. It'll tell you everything you're doing wrong, and everything you're doing right. And the exam will be wrapped in love.

Apply yourself to the whole text, and apply the whole text to yourself.

JOHANNES ALBRECHT BENGEL

Meditation's Importance

Make me to understand the way of thy precepts:
so shall I talk of thy wondrous works.

PSALMS 119:27 (KJV)

Meditating on God's Word will help to blow away clouds of confusion and misunderstandings about spiritual things.

More people are troubled by what is plain in Scripture than by what is obscure.

ROY L. SMITH

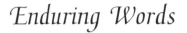

Enduring Words

"But the word of the LORD endures forever."
Now this is the word which by the gospel was
preached to you.

1 PETER 1:25 (NKJV)

Many people have tried to stop the power of the
Bible but it's impossible. God's Words will last forever—just like Him.

Voltaire said, "Another century and there will not
be a Bible on earth." Voltaire is gone and the Bible
is still the best selling book in the world.

KATHY COLLARD MILLER

Not Forsaken

Those who know your name will trust in you,
for you, LORD, have never forsaken those who
seek you.

PSALMS 9:10 (NIV)

No matter how far you stray from God, it only takes seeking Him again to restore your relationship with Him.

None of us ever desired anything more ardently than God desires to bring men to a knowledge of himself.

JOHANNES TAULER

Fighting Fear

He will cover you with his feathers, and under
his wings you will find refuge; his faithfulness
will be your shield and rampart. You will not
fear the terror of night, nor the arrow that flies
by day, nor the pestilence that stalks in the
darkness, nor the plague that destroys at
midday.

PSALMS 91:4–6 (NIV)

When fear steals your trust in God's promises, re-
hearse the truth about God. It'll be like a bullet proof
vest is suddenly protecting your heart from fear.

God rules in realms to which he is admitted.

MARY WELCH

Trust In Jesus

Some trust in chariots and some in horses, but
we trust in the name of the LORD our God.

PSALMS 20:7 (NIV)

The only person or thing who will not disappoint
us is God.

He who is disappointed in himself is he who first
trusted in himself.

ANONYMOUS

Anxious For Nothing

Be anxious for nothing, but in everything by
prayer and supplication, with thanksgiving, let
your requests be made known to God;

PHILIPPIANS 4:6 (NKJV)

There is absolutely nothing that is worthy to be anxious about when you know God loves you.

Worry, like a rocking chair, will give you something to do, but it won't get you anywhere.

VANCE HAVNER

Well-Placed Trust

. . . in God I trust; I will not be afraid. What can man do to me?

PSALMS 56:11 (NIV)

We can evaluate how much we're trusting God by our level of fear or anxiety.

He who offers to God a second place offers him no place.

JOHN RUSKIN

Abandon Your Own Understanding

*Trust in the LORD with all thine heart; and
lean not unto thine own understanding. In all
thy ways acknowledge him, and he shall direct
thy paths.*

PROVERBS 3:5–6 (KJV)

If you're leaning on the fence of your own understanding, watch out! The fence will fall over. Lean
instead on the solid brick wall of God's perspective.

Since Jesus became my Supreme Programmer, he
has kept the scanner and memory tapes moving
rapidly and with a minimum of downtime.

DONALD R. BROWN

Results Of Dependence On God

"Because he loves me," says the LORD, "I will rescue him; I will protect him, for he acknowledges my name. He will call upon me, and I will answer him; I will be with him in trouble, I will deliver him and honor him. With long life will I satisfy him and show him my salvation."

PSALMS 91:14–16 (NIV)

Depending on God brings many wonderful results, like satisfaction, honor, deliverance, and salvation.

For God to explain a trial would be to destroy its object, which is that of calling forth simple faith and implicit obedience.

ALFRED EDERSHEIM

Truth

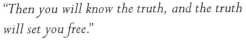

*"Then you will know the truth, and the truth
will set you free."*

JOHN 8:32 (NIV)

Looking at life from God's perspective sets you free
from all sorts of wrong assumptions.

When life becomes all snarled up, offer it to our
Lord and let Him untie the knots.

A BOOK OF DAYS FOR CHRISTIANS

Righteous Wisdom

*But the wisdom that is from above is first pure,
then peaceable, gentle, willing to yield, full of
mercy and good fruits, without partiality and
without hypocrisy. Now the fruit of righteousness is sown in peace by those who make peace.*

JAMES 3:17–18 (NKJV)

If you're wondering whether your mindset is God's
wisdom, evaluate it from His perspective.

A wise man sees as much as he ought, not as much
as he can.

MICHEL DE MONTAIGNE

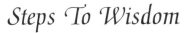

Steps To Wisdom

The fear of the LORD is the beginning of
wisdom: a good understanding have all they
that do his commandments: his praise endureth
for ever.

PSALMS 111:10 (KJV)

Gaining wisdom is a process; keep taking step after step of seeking God and you'll build up lots of wisdom muscles.

It doesn't matter how much money you have; everyone has to buy wisdom on the installment plan.

CRIT

Generous Wisdom

If any of you lacks wisdom, he should ask God,
who gives generously to all without finding
fault, and it will be given to him.

JAMES 1:5 (NIV)

You don't have to ask more than once for wisdom.
God can't wait to give it to you.

Knowledge is horizontal. Wisdom is vertical—it
comes down from above.

BILLY GRAHAM

Importance Of Memorization

I have taken your words to heart so I would not sin against you.

PSALMS 119:11 (NCV)

Memorizing God's Word, His Love Letter to us, is the source of everything needed to prevent sin from overwhelming us.

When you read God's Word, you must constantly be saying to yourself, "It is talking to me, and about me."

SOREN KIERKEGAARD

Good Judgment

Teach me good discernment and knowledge, For
I believe in Thy commandments.

PSALMS 119:66 (NASB)

Following God's ideas gives us a foundation of wisdom and understanding. What a blessed motivation for reading the Bible.

No one ever graduates from Bible study until he meets its Author face to face.

EVERETT HARRIS

True Disciple

To the Jews who had believed him, Jesus said, "If you hold to my teaching, you are really my disciples."

JOHN 8:31 (NIV)

Have you wondered what a disciple of Jesus really is? It's a person who makes the Bible their greatest source for living.

Bible study is like eating peanuts. The more you eat, the more you want to eat.

PAUL LITTLE

Opened Eyes

*Open my eyes that I may see wonderful things
in your law.*

PSALMS 119:18 (NIV)

Sometimes the Bible seems confusing, but if we'll
ask for understanding, God will give it.

Unless we form the habit of going to the Bible in
bright moments as well as in trouble, we cannot
fully respond to its consolations because we lack
equilibrium between light and darkness.

HELEN KELLER

All-Purpose Word Of God

*All Scripture is God-breathed and is useful for
teaching, rebuking, correcting and training in
righteousness, so that the man of God may be
thoroughly equipped for every good work.*
2 TIMOTHY 3:16–17 (NIV)

God's Word, the Bible, is powerful. It trains, em-
powers and teaches.

God did not give us the Scriptures to increase our
knowledge, but to change our lives.
D.L. MOODY

Bible Knowledge

*Those who love Thy law have great peace, And
nothing causes them to stumble.*

PSALMS 119:165 (NASB)

If you don't know God's thinking through His Word,
you may find yourself stumbling down the road of
life. Put on the glasses of knowledge in the Bible.

The Bible is God's chart for you to steer by, to keep
you from the bottom of the sea, and to show you
where the harbor is, and how to reach it without
running on rocks or bars.

HENRY WARD BEECHER

Other Books by Starburst Publishers

(Partial listing—full list available on request)
www.starburstpublishers.com

Promises of God's Abundance—Kathy Collard Miller

Subtitled: *For a More Meaningful Life.* The perfect gift book filled with Scripture, questions for growth and a Simple Thought for the Day will guide you to an abundant and more meaningful life.

(trade paper)   ISBN 0914984098   **$9.95**

God's Abundance—Edited by Kathy Collard Miller

Let God's Word lead you to a simpler, yet more abundant life in this day-by-day inspirational. This is a collection of thoughts by Christian writers such as Patsy Clairmont and Tony Evans.

(hardcover)   ISBN 0914984977   **$19.95**

God's Unexpected Blessings—Edited by Kathy Collard Miller

Witness God at work and learn to see the *Unexpected Blessings* in life through essays by Christian writers such as Billy Graham and Barbara Johnson.

(hardcover)   ISBN 0914984071   **$18.95**

Why Fret That God Stuff?—Compiled by Kathy Collard Miller

Subtitled: *Stories of Encouragement to Help You Let Go and Let God Take Control of All Things in Your Life* is the perfect beginning to finding joy and peace for the real world! Learn as others like Billy Graham and Barbara Johnson share openly their own experiences of living life more productively.

(trade paper)   ISBN 0914984500   **$12.95**

If I Only Knew . . . What Would Jesus Do?—Joan Hake Robie

This book looks at everyday problems through the lens of the fundamental teachings of Jesus.

(trade paper)   ISBN 091498439X   **$9.95**

Books By Starburst Publishers Cont'd.

Conversations with God the Father—Mark R. Littleton
  Subtitled: *Encounters with the One True God*. Contemplate the nature of God with fictional answers
  to questions as God might answer them.
  (hardcover)   ISBN 0914984195   **$17.95**

The Fragile Thread—Aliske Webb
  This touching fictional story traces a woman's journey of transformation. After Aggie reaches
  mid-life alone, she decides to leave her practice in the city and open a quilt shop in a small
  town. In the process, she rediscovers her values, beliefs, and spiritual foundation.
  (hardcover)   ISBN 0914984543   **$17.95**

Revelation—God's Word for the Biblically-Inept™—Daymond R. Duck
  The first in a new series designed to make understanding and learning the Bible as easy and fun as
  learning your ABC's.
  (trade paper)   ISBN 0914984985   **$16.95**

Daniel—God's Word for the Biblically-Inept™—Daymond R. Duck
  Daniel—God's Word for the Biblically-Inept™ is the second book in this *Revolutionary Commentary*™
  series. Author Daymond Duck makes the Book of Daniel much less overwhelming.
  (trade paper)   ISBN 0914984489   **$16.95**

The Bible—God's Word for the Biblically-Inept™—Larry Richards
  The Bible—God's Word for the Biblically-Inept™ is the third book in this *Revolutionary
  Commentary*™ series. Bible expert Larry Richards breaks down the Bible into easy-to-
  understand pieces for all types of readers.
  (trade paper)   ISBN 0914984551   **$16.95**

Purchasing Information:

Books are available from your favorite bookstore, either from current stock or special order. To assist a bookstore in
locating your selection, be sure to give title, author, and ISBN #. If unable to purchase from a bookstore, you may
order direct from STARBURST PUBLISHERS by mail, phone, fax, or through our secure website at
www.starburstpublishers.com. When ordering enclose full payment plus $3.00 for shipping and handling ($4.00 if
Canada or overseas). Payment in U.S. Funds only. Please allow two to three weeks minimum (longer overseas) for
delivery. Make checks payable to and mail to: STARBURST PUBLISHERS, P.O. Box 4123, LANCASTER, PA 17604.
Credit card orders may also be placed by calling 1-800-441-1456 (credit card orders only), Mon-Fri, 8:30 a.m.—5:30
p.m. Eastern Standard Time. Prices subject to change without notice. Catalog available for a 9x12 self-addressed
envelope with 4 first-class stamps. 11-98